CLEVELAND BROWNS

BY TOM GLAVE

The Child's World

Published by The Child's World®
1980 Lookout Drive • Mankato, MN 56003-1705
800-599-READ • www.childsworld.com

Acknowledgments
The Child's World®: Mary Berendes, Publishing Director
Red Line Editorial: Editorial direction
The Design Lab: Design
Amnet: Production

Design Element: Dean Bertoncelj/Shutterstock Images
Photographs ©: Tom DiPace/AP Images, cover; Jeff
Haynes/AP Images, 5, 7; Ron Schwane/AP Images, 9;
AJ Mast/AP Images, 11; Jerry Sharp/Shutterstock Images,
13; Amy Sancetta/AP Images, 14–15; MBD/AP Images, 17;
Mark Duncan/AP Images, 19; NFL Photos/AP Images,
21; AP Images, 23, 29; Kellen MIcah/Icon Sportswire, 25;
Scott A. Miller/AP Images, 27

ISBN 9781631439933
LCCN 2014959698

Printed in the United States of America
Mankato, MN
July, 2015
PA02265

ABOUT THE AUTHOR

Tom Glave grew up watching football on TV and playing it in the field next to his house. He learned to write about sports at the University of Missouri–Columbia and has written for newspapers in New Jersey, Missouri, Arkansas, and Texas. He lives near Houston, Texas, and cannot wait to play backyard football with his kids Tommy, Lucas, and Allison.

TABLE OF CONTENTS

GO, BROWNS!	4
WHO ARE THE BROWNS?	6
WHERE THEY CAME FROM	8
WHO THEY PLAY	10
WHERE THEY PLAY	12
THE FOOTBALL FIELD	14
BIG DAYS	16
TOUGH DAYS	18
MEET THE FANS	20
HEROES THEN	22
HEROES NOW	24
GEARING UP	26
SPORTS STATS	28
GLOSSARY	30
FIND OUT MORE	31
INDEX	32

GO, BROWNS!

The Cleveland Browns had early success. They won seven **league** championships from 1946 to 1955. But they could not keep winning. The Browns struggled for years. Then the team moved. The Browns headed to Baltimore after the 1995 season. Football returned to Cleveland in 1999. The new team has not done very well. It has been hard on the fans. But they still show up to games. Let's meet the Browns.

Wide receiver Andrew Hawkins runs with the ball in a game against the Baltimore Ravens on September 21, 2014.

WHO ARE THE BROWNS?

The Cleveland Browns play in the National Football League (NFL). They are one of the 32 teams in the NFL. The NFL includes the American Football Conference (AFC) and the National Football Conference (NFC). The winner of the AFC plays the winner of the NFC in the **Super Bowl**. The Browns play in the North Division of the AFC. They have never played in the Super Bowl. But they did win eight championships before the Super Bowl began after the 1966 season.

Running backs Isaiah Crowell (34) and Terrance West celebrate a touchdown in a game against the Indianapolis Colts on December 7, 2014.

WHERE THEY CAME FROM

The Browns began playing in 1946. Fans named the team in honor of Paul Brown. He was Cleveland's first coach. The Browns first played in the All-America Football Conference (AAFC). They won four AAFC Championships. The league ended after the 1949 season. So the Browns joined the NFL. They won three NFL Championships in their first six years. Owner Art Modell wanted a new stadium in the 1990s. The city of Cleveland did not build one. So he moved the team to Baltimore in 1995. It became the Baltimore Ravens. The Browns name and history stayed in Cleveland. A new Browns team was created in 1999.

Fans were excited to have the Browns back in Cleveland when the team returned for the 1999 season.

WHO THEY PLAY

The Cleveland Browns play 16 games each season. With so few games, each one is important. Every year, the Cleveland Browns play two games against each of the other three teams in their division. Those teams are the Pittsburgh Steelers, Baltimore Ravens, and Cincinnati Bengals. The Browns also play six other teams from the AFC and four from the NFC. Cleveland and Pittsburgh share the AFC's oldest **rivalry**. The Browns and Bengals both play in Ohio. Many fans of both teams are usually at those games. Cleveland fans are still upset about the team's move to Baltimore. That makes the Browns and Ravens rivals, too.

Fans in Ohio love watching the Bengals and Browns battle on the football field.

WHERE THEY PLAY

The original Browns team played at Cleveland Municipal Stadium. It was torn down when the Browns left for Baltimore. FirstEnergy Stadium is Cleveland's home now. It was built in 1998. It sits on the same ground as the Browns' old stadium. FirstEnergy Stadium holds 68,000 fans. The seats behind the east end zone are called "The Dawg Pound." They are usually filled with crazy fans. The stadium is located on the shore of Lake Erie. It is next to the Rock and Roll Hall of Fame.

Cleveland Browns Stadium became known as FirstEnergy Stadium in 2013.

THE FOOTBALL FIELD

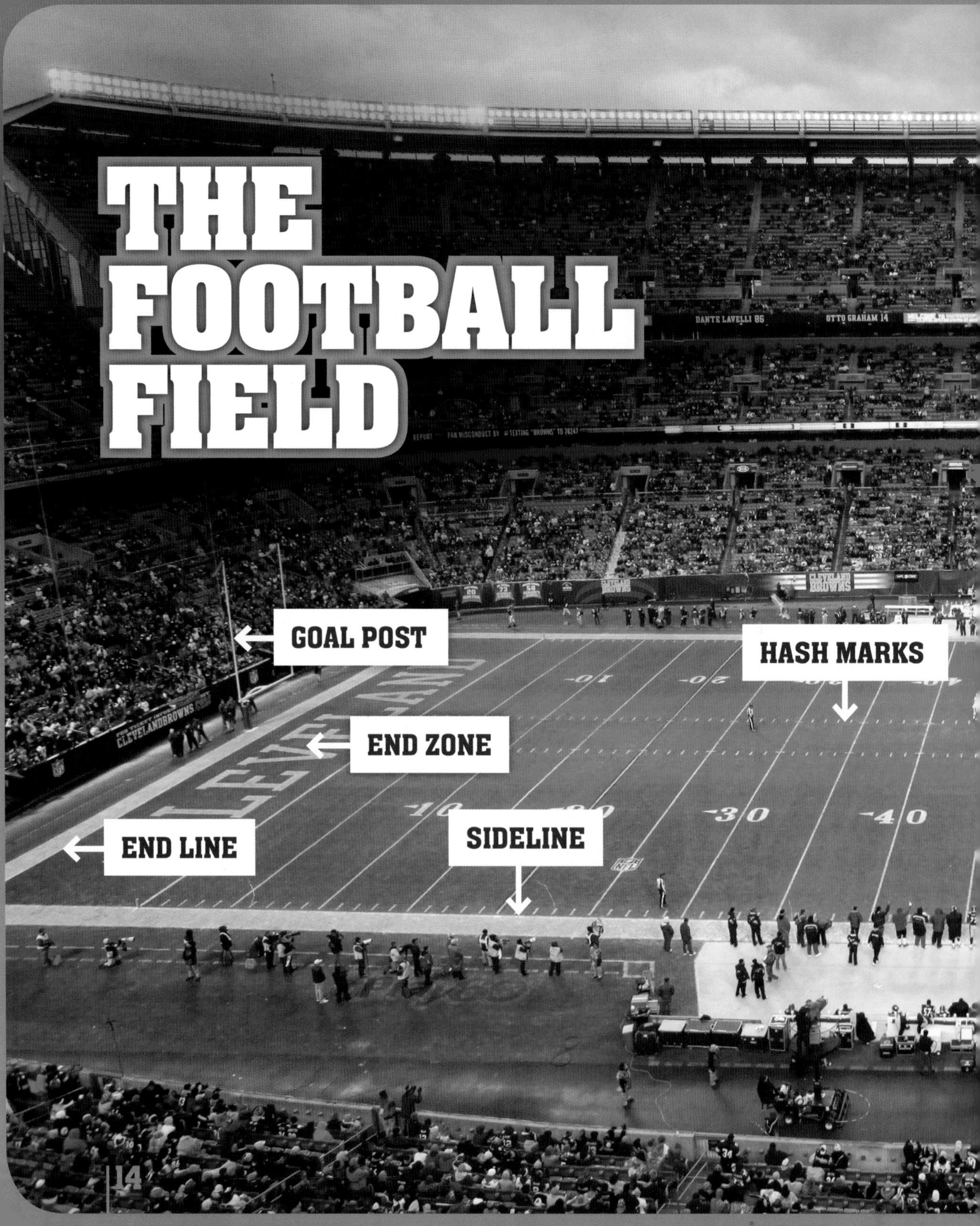
GOAL POST
HASH MARKS
END ZONE
END LINE
SIDELINE
DANTE LAVELLI 86
OTTO GRAHAM 14
CLEVELAND

MIDFIELD

20-YARD LINE

GOAL LINE

BENCH AREA

BIG DAYS

The Browns have had some great moments in their history. Here are three of the greatest:

1964—The Browns won their eighth league title. They beat the Baltimore Colts 27-0 on December 27. Jim Brown had a great regular season. He rushed for 1,446 yards. That led the NFL. He had 114 yards in the championship game.

1980—Cleveland had a lot of close calls. Twelve of its sixteen regular-season games were decided by seven points or fewer. The team was nicknamed "The Kardiac Kids." The Browns finished 11–5. That won them the AFC Central. Quarterback Brian Sipe was the NFL **Most Valuable Player (MVP)**.

Quarterback Brian Sipe (17) had the best year of his career in 1980, leading "The Kardiac Kids" to an AFC Central title.

2002—The **playoffs** returned to Cleveland. The Browns went 9-7. They won their final two regular-season games. That got the Browns into the postseason. It was the team's first playoff appearance since the NFL came back to Cleveland.

TOUGH DAYS

Football is a hard game. Even the best teams have rough games and seasons. Here are some of the toughest times in Browns history:

1975—The Browns started the season 0-9. That is the team's worst start through 2014. They gave up at least 40 points in three straight games. Cleveland finished the season 3-11.

1988—Cleveland played the Denver Broncos on January 17. It was the AFC Championship Game. The game was tied with 1:12 left. Browns running back Earnest Byner took a handoff. He was about to score. But he **fumbled** just before the goal line. It is known as "The Fumble." The Broncos ended up winning 38-33.

Running back Earnest Byner's fumble is one of the most famous plays in Browns history.

Denver had beaten Cleveland late in the AFC title game the year before, too.

1995—In November, Browns owner Art Modell told the team it was heading to Baltimore. The Browns then lost six straight games. Fans ripped out pieces of the stadium after the last home game.

MEET THE FANS

A great group of fans called "The Dawg Pound" loves the Browns. Cleveland's defense was nicknamed "Dawgs" before the 1985 season. Fans started barking to cheer for them. Now some fans wear dog masks to games. Cleveland has two dog mascots. Chomps is a humanlike Labrador. He wears a football jersey and helmet. Swagger is a real Bullmastiff. Swagger runs onto the field before home games. The Browns Backers are Cleveland fans around the world. They watch games together in foreign countries.

Fans in "The Dawg Pound" are some of the most famous in the NFL.

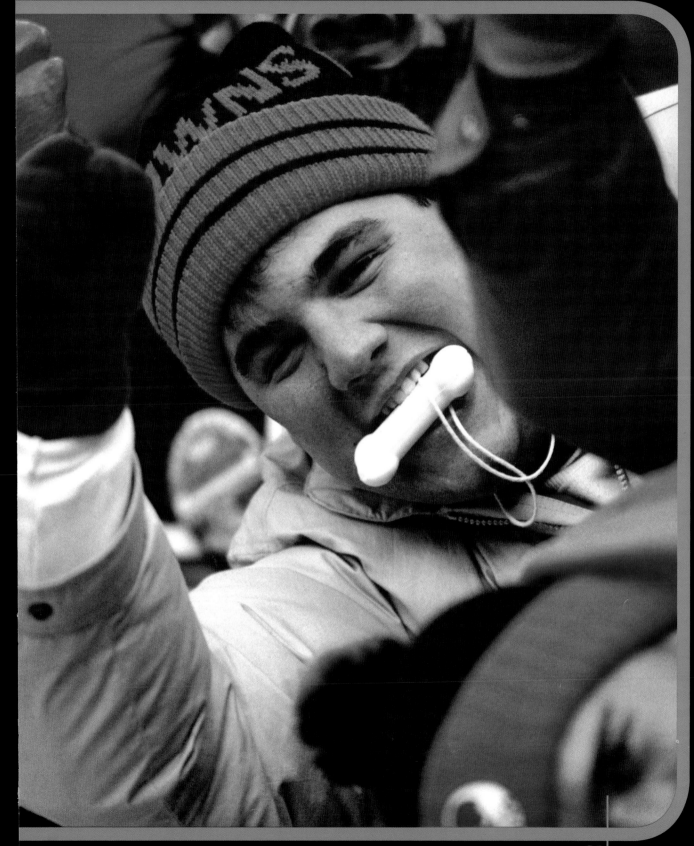

HEROES THEN

Otto Graham was the Browns' first quarterback. He helped Cleveland dominate. Graham threw four touchdown passes in the 1950 NFL Championship Game. He then threw three touchdown passes and ran for three more in the 1954 NFL Championship Game. Jim Brown is one of the greatest NFL running backs. He led the league in rushing in eight of his nine seasons in Cleveland. Brown was the NFL **Rookie** of the Year in 1957. He also was the NFL MVP three times. Lou Groza was with Cleveland from 1946 to 1959 and 1961 to 1967. He played on the offensive line and kicked. Groza made nine Pro Bowls. Those three players are all in the Pro Football Hall of Fame.

Quarterback Otto Graham, who also played defensive back, was named MVP in 1951, 1953, and 1955.

HEROES NOW

Cornerback Joe Haden locks down receivers. He had six interceptions as a rookie in 2010. Haden earned his first Pro Bowl selection in 2013. Offensive lineman Joe Thomas was picked third in the 2007 **NFL Draft**. He made the Pro Bowl in each of his first eight seasons. He did not miss a single offensive snap in any of those years. Wide receiver Andrew Hawkins joined the Browns in 2014. He led the team with 824 receiving yards that year. Defensive back Tashaun Gipson had six interceptions in 2014.

Tackle Joe Thomas has been considered one of the best offensive linemen in the NFL since entering the league in 2007.

GEARING UP

NFL players wear team uniforms. They wear helmets and pads to keep them safe. Cleats help them make quick moves and run fast. Some players wear extra gear for protection.

THE FOOTBALL

NFL footballs are made of leather. Under the leather is a lining that fills with air to give the ball its shape. The leather has bumps or "pebbles." These help players grip the ball. Laces help players control their throws. Footballs are also called "pigskins" because some of the first balls were made from pig bladders. Today they are made of leather from cows.

Defensive back Tashaun Gipson had at least five interceptions in each of his first two seasons as a regular starter.

HELMET

SHOULDER PADS

GLOVES

THIGH PADS

FOOTBALL

SPORTS STATS

Here are some of the all-time career records for the Cleveland Browns. All the stats are through the 2014 season.

RUSHING YARDS

Jim Brown 12,312

Leroy Kelly 7,274

RECEPTIONS

Ozzie Newsome 662

Dante Lavelli 386

PASSING YARDS

Brian Sipe 23,713

Otto Graham 23,584

INTERCEPTIONS

Thom Darden 45

Warren Lahr 44

SACKS

Clay Matthews 62

Michael Dean Perry 51.5

POINTS

Lou Groza 1,608

Phil Dawson 1,271

Running back Jim Brown, who left the game as one of the NFL's best players, retired with a career-record 12,312 rushing yards.

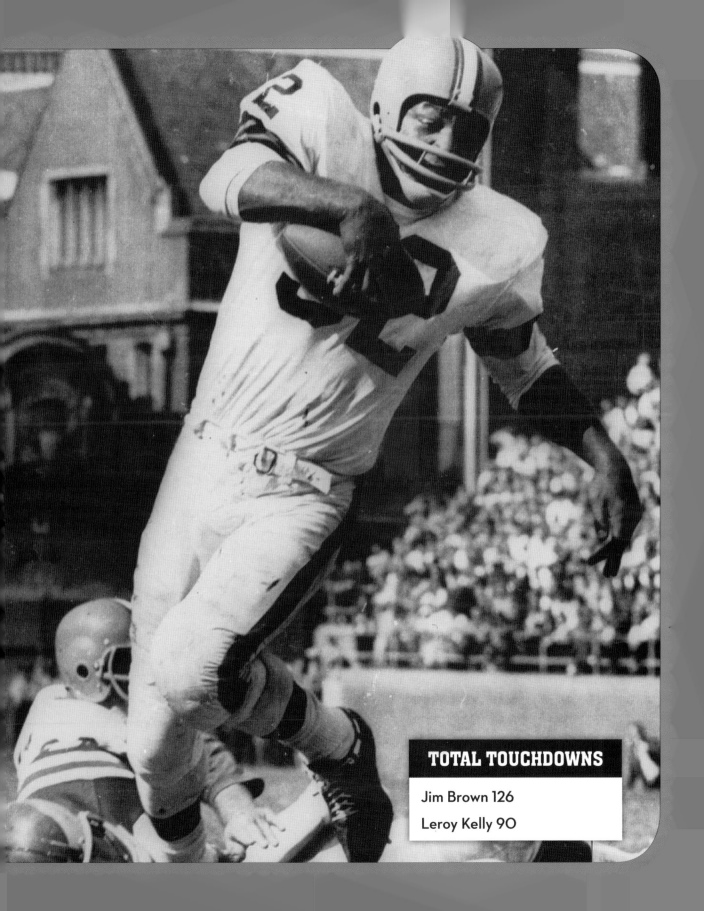

TOTAL TOUCHDOWNS

Jim Brown 126

Leroy Kelly 90

GLOSSARY

fumbled when a player lost control of the football and the other team got it

league an organization of sports teams that compete against each other

Most Valuable Player (MVP) a yearly award given to the top player in the NFL

NFL Draft a meeting of all the NFL teams at which they choose college players to join them

playoffs a series of games after the regular season that decides which two teams play in the Super Bowl

rivalry an ongoing competition between teams that play each other often, over a long time

rookie a player playing in his first season

Super Bowl the championship game of the NFL, played between the winners of the AFC and the NFC

FIND OUT MORE

IN THE LIBRARY

Gigliotti, Jim. *Super Bowl Super Teams.*
New York: Scholastic, 2010.

Gilbert, Sara. *The Story of the Cleveland Browns.*
Mankato, MN: Creative Education, 2014.

Grossi, Tony. *Tales from the Cleveland Browns
Sideline.* New York: Sports Publishing, 2012.

ON THE WEB

Visit our Web site for links about the Cleveland Browns:
childsworld.com/links

*Note to Parents, Teachers, and Librarians: We routinely verify our Web links to make
sure they are safe and active sites. So encourage your readers to check them out!*

INDEX

AAFC Championship, 8
AFC North, 6, 10
All-America Football
 Conference (AAFC), 8
American Football
 Conference (AFC), 6, 10, 16,
 18, 19

Baltimore Colts, 16
Baltimore Ravens, 8, 10
Brown, Jim, 16, 20
Brown, Paul, 8
Browns Backers, The, 20
Byner, Earnest, 18

Chomps (mascot), 20
Cincinnati Bengals, 10

"Dawg Pound, The," 12, 20
Denver Broncos, 18
"Drive, The," 19

FirstEnergy Stadium, 12
"Fumble, The," 18

Gipson, Tashaun, 24
Graham, Otto, 22
Groza, Lou, 22

Haden, Joe, 24
Hawkins, Andrew, 24

"Kardiac Kids, The," 16

Modell, Art, 8, 19

National Football Conference
 (NFC), 6, 10
National Football League
 (NFL), 6, 8, 16, 17, 20, 24
NFL Championship, 6, 8, 16, 20

Pittsburgh Steelers, 10

Sipe, Brian, 16
Super Bowl, 6
Swagger (mascot), 20

Thomas, Joe, 24